AWESOME ACTIVITIES

CRAZY CONTRAPTIONS

Susan Martineau

Illustrations by Martin Ursell

WINDMILL
BOOKS

New York

Published in 2012 by Windmill Books, LLC
303 Park Avenue South, Suite #1280, New York, NY 10010-3657

Adaptations to North American Edition © 2012 Windmill Books, LLC
© 2012 b small publishing ltd

Library of Congress Cataloging-in-Publication Data

Martineau, Susan.
Crazy contraptions / by Susan Martineau. — 1st ed.
p. cm. — (Awesome activities)
Includes index.
ISBN 978-1-61533-367-7 (library binding) — ISBN 978-1-61533-405-6 (pbk.) — ISBN 978-1-61533-467-4 (6-pack)
1. Scientific recreation—Juvenile literature. I. Title.
Q164.M27537 2012
607.8—dc22
2010052114

Manufactured in the United States of America

CPSIA Compliance Information: Batch #BS2011WM: For Further Information contact Windmill Books, New York, New York at 1-866-478-0556

Contents

Before You Begin

Most of the contraptions in this book are made with old stuff you will have around the house already. Don't forget to cover work surfaces with newspaper before you start. Remember to clean up afterward, too!

You will need a bit of grown-up help in one or two places. These have been marked with this special symbol. !

Air Power

Blast Off!

This balloon rocket really whizzes along. You can use the same balloon again and again to show it off to your friends. You'll need a friend standing by to help set up the launch.

What you will need:
- 7 feet (2 m) of string
- Tape
- Drinking straw
- Clothespin
- Chair
- Balloon

1

2

3

Thread the string through the straw. Tie one end to a door handle and the other to a chair.

Place the chair so that the string is taut. Blow up the balloon and clip it closed.

Get a friend to help you tape the balloon to the straw. Now unclip the balloon and watch it go!

It's a Fact!

Isaac Newton's Third Law of Motion says that for every action there is an equal and opposite reaction. In this case, the air is pushed out of the back of the balloon and this action makes the balloon move forwards, the opposite reaction.

In a real rocket, fuel burns and makes hot gases which come rushing out of the back of the rocket. This propels the rocket upwards.

You could tape a small box under the balloon for carrying "cargo." An empty matchbox would be ideal.

Funky Fountains

Here are some fun fountains to make with your friends. Make a few and have a competition to see whose is best. You could add some food coloring to the water for extra fun. It's a good idea to do this outside!

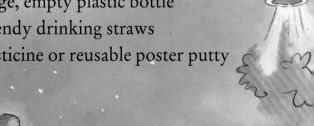

1 Remove any labels from the bottle. Fill the bottle halfway with water.

2 Put one straw into the water and position the other one so it is just above the water. Put some plasticine or poster putty tightly around the mouth to make an airtight seal.

3 Put the bottle into a sink or take it outside. Now blow into the straw which is not in the water.

Blow!

See how powerful air can be by blowing through a straw at a paper boat!

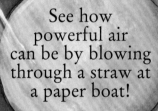

Rocket Man

Wernher von Braun (1912–1977) was a German inventor who longed to send a rocket to the Moon. Unfortunately, during World War II (1939–1945), he was ordered to design rocket bombs instead. After the war, he went to work in the United States and by the 1960s he was working at NASA. He led the team that launched the Saturn rockets which first took men to the moon.

It's a Fact!

When you blow air through a straw, it squashes the air up, or compresses it. This makes the air more powerful. The air you blow into the bottle pushes the water up through the other straw.

Mighty Robot

Although this robot friend will not wash your dishes or clean up your room, he's fun to have around and will hold stuff for you. You can really get creative when adding buttons and features to your robot. These are just some ideas to get you started.

What you will need:
- 1 medium-sized box
- 1 small box
- Aluminum foil
- Tape
- 6 toilet paper tubes
- Scissors
- 3 glittery pipe cleaners
- Sequins
- Glue
- Old pieces of styrofoam packing
- Small bottle caps
- Old, shiny candy wrappers

1

Cover both of the boxes with foil as if you were wrapping a present. Use tape to secure the foil.

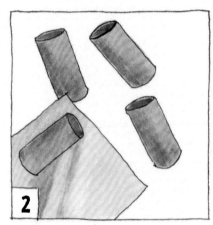

2

Cover four of the toilet paper tubes with foil and tuck the foil inside the ends.

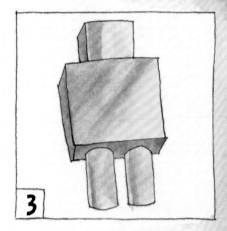

3

Tape the small box to the top of the medium one. Then tape two of the covered tubes underneath for legs.

It's a Fact!

Robots are used in many industries in factory production lines. But they don't look at all like the artificial humans, or androids, you see in movies! They're really useful, though, and can do jobs that humans would find very boring. In car manufacturing, robots weld together the steel panels to make the car body and then spray the body with several coats of paint.

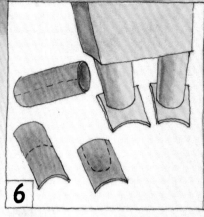

4 Cut two sections about 1.5 inches (4 cm) long from the ends of a remaining tube. Cover these with foil. Tuck in the ends.

Tape these to the other two covered tubes to form hands. Now tape these arms to the robot's body.

❗

7 With adult help, use the scissors to pierce 3 holes in the top of the head.

Cut the remaining tube in half lengthwise. Cut two feet as shown. Cover these with foil. Tape them to the legs.

8 Curl the pipe cleaners around your finger and then push them through the holes.

9 Glue on sequins for eyes. Cover a piece of rectangular styrofoam with foil and stick it on to make a mouth.

10 Cover bottle caps with foil and candy wrappers. Stick them on for buttons.

11 Use the arms and hands to hold pens, pencils, or even your toothbrush!

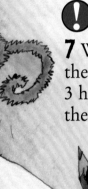

Androids in the Future?

Scientists are researching ways to make robots that can think for themselves and not have to be programed before they perform certain tasks. Maybe one day you might have a robot around the house who will do the dishes without having to be nagged!

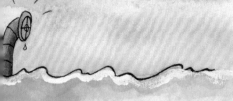

Spyscope

Make a nifty **periscope** for peering over the fence at your neighbors! The sort of mirrors you need are small make-up ones which you can get from drugstores.

What you will need:

- 1 long, thin box, about 10 inches (24 cm) long and 2.5 inches (6 cm) wide
- Scissors and tape
- 2 small rectangular mirrors, about 2.5 inches (6 cm) by 3 inches (8 cm)

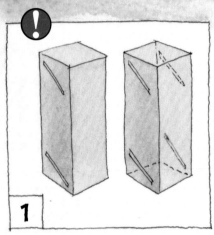

1 Cut two slanting slits on one side of the box. Turn it over and cut two more. These should line up with the first slits.

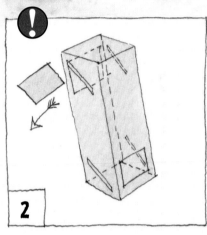

2 Cut two rectangular windows in the box, as shown. They should line up with the slits.

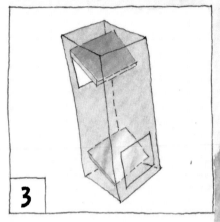

3 Slide the mirrors through the slits so that their reflective sides are facing each other. Use tape to hold them in place.

4 Hold one window to your eyes and look through it. What can you see?

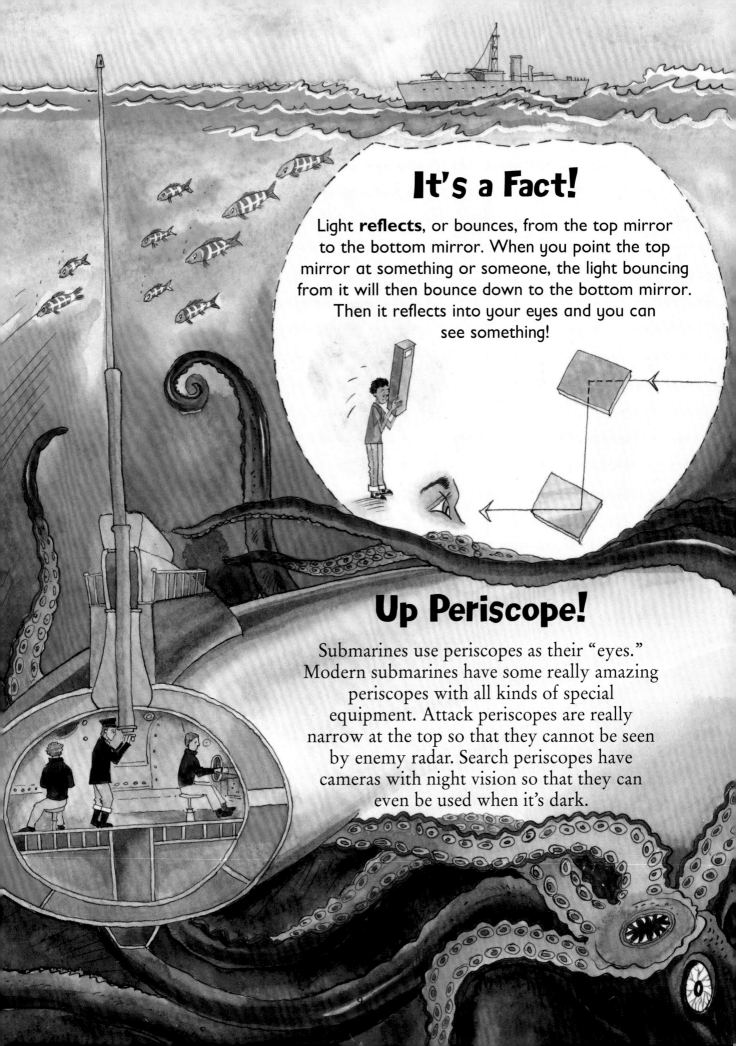

It's a Fact!

Light **reflects**, or bounces, from the top mirror to the bottom mirror. When you point the top mirror at something or someone, the light bouncing from it will then bounce down to the bottom mirror. Then it reflects into your eyes and you can see something!

Up Periscope!

Submarines use periscopes as their "eyes." Modern submarines have some really amazing periscopes with all kinds of special equipment. Attack periscopes are really narrow at the top so that they cannot be seen by enemy radar. Search periscopes have cameras with night vision so that they can even be used when it's dark.

Anchors Aweigh!

Make yourself a speedy trimaran that will skim along in a breeze! Next try making another boat, such as a catamaran.

What you will need:

- 1 large, thin piece of styrofoam from food packaging
- Marker
- Scissors
- Tape
- 4 wooden skewers, about 10 inches (25 cm) long
- 10 inches (24 cm) by 5 inches (12 cm) of very thin fabric
- Thread

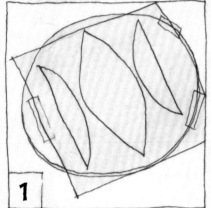

1

Draw the three shapes seen here on the styrofoam with a marker. Then cut them out.

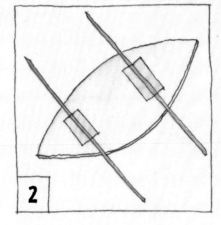

2

Tape two skewers across the center of the main hull as seen here.

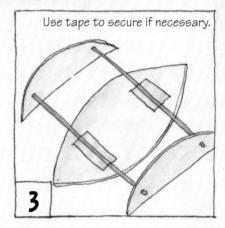

Use tape to secure if necessary.

3

Hold the side hulls with their curved sides up and gently push them onto the ends of the skewers.

4

Cut the fabric into two triangles. Insert skewers as seen. Tie an 8-inch (20 cm) piece of thread to each free corner.

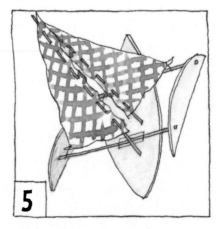

5

Push these skewers into the main hull. Tie the loose threads to the horizontal skewers.

6

Tape the two upright skewers together at the top. You're ready to sail!

Monohulls and Hydrofoils

Drag is the force that slows a boat down when it's moving through the water. The less hull a boat has in the water, the faster it can go.

A monohull is a boat with one hull. A normal sailing yacht is a monohull and can sail at up to 22 miles per hour (35 km/h).

A catamaran has two hulls. When the wind blows strongly, it can lean and balance on one hull and move as fast as 34 miles per hour (55 km/h).

A trimaran has three hulls, one main hull and two floats. In high winds, it can speed along on one float at up to 37 miles per hour (60 km/h).

A hydrofoil has three hulls and amazing slanting runners under the side hulls. When the wind gets up, all three hulls can be lifted out of the water and the boat speeds along on these runners at up to 41 miles per hour (66 km/h).

11

Weather Station

Be a weather scientist with this handy **barometer** and **rain gauge**. The barometer will tell you what the air pressure is like and you'll be able to see how this predicts whether it rains or not! Why not keep a record of your findings in a notebook?

Handy Barometer

If you can't find clear tubing or straws, then use a regular straw. The food coloring will help you see the level of the water through the straw.

What you will need:
- Clear glass or plastic jar
- Tape and ruler
- 8-inch (20 cm) clear plastic tube or drinking straw
- Food coloring
- Reusable poster putty

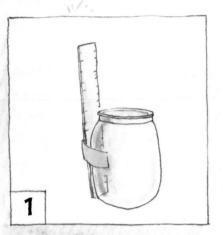

1

Tape the ruler upright on the outside of the jar.

2

Fill the jar halfway with cold water. Then add a few drops of food coloring.

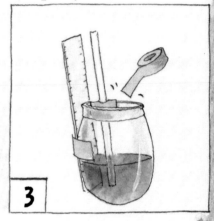

3

Tape the tube or straw to the inside of the jar. It should not touch the bottom.

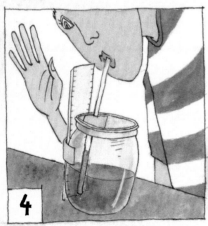

4

Suck some water halfway up the tube. Pinch the tube. Cap the top with poster putty.

Keep your barometer indoors. Make sure it is not in a chilly or sunny place. Note the level of the water in the tube each day. Record the day's weather, too.

Rain Catcher

This rain gauge can be hung up over a fence or balcony. Make sure it isn't underneath any overhanging bits of building or roof or under any trees. Note the level of the water each day in your notebook.

What you will need:
- Clean, empty jar (preferably with straight sides)
- Plastic ruler
- Reusable poster putty
- Old wire hanger

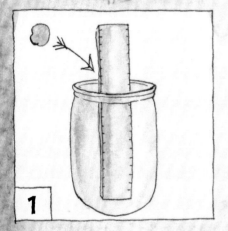

1

2

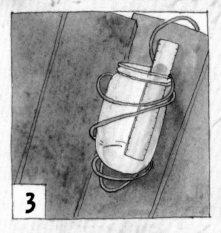

3

Place the ruler inside the jar. Secure it to the side of the jar with the poster putty.

Ask a grown-up to help you untwist the wire coathanger and then curl it around the jar.

Make sure the wire goes underneath the jar. Finish off with a curl that you can use to hang the rain gauge.

It's a Fact!

How does your beaker barometer work?

When the pressure in the **atmosphere** goes up, the water in the barometer jar is forced downwards. This will push the water in the tube or straw upwards. You will see that happening if you check the level against the ruler. Rising atmospheric pressure means that we should have clear or sunny weather.

If the water in the tube is going down this is because the air pressure is going down. It could be bringing some cloudy or rainy weather with it.

Snap Happy

See how a camera works by making this simple device. You'll need a friend to help you.

What you will need:
- Old shoebox
- Thick black paint and a paintbrush
- Pin
- Tracing paper
- Scissors
- Tape
- Large, adult-sized coat

Don't make the hole too big.

1

Take the lid off the shoebox. Paint the inside black and leave it to dry. Use the pin to make a hole in the middle of the bottom of the box.

2

Cut out a large piece of tracing paper to fit across the open side of the box with about 1 inch (2 cm) to spare on all sides.

3

Tape the paper firmly around all the sides of the box so that it is stretched tightly across the open side.

Camera Obscura

Camera obscura means "dark chamber" in Latin. The pinhole camera is a camera obscura on a small scale. However, whole rooms can be made into dark chambers. Artists and astronomers over the centuries have observed images from the outside world through a pinhole of light coming into a specially darkened room.

4 Now you are ready to try out your camera. Take the box and coat outside because it will work best in bright light. (If you are inside, point it toward a light or lamp.)

7 Point the pinhole side of the box at a building, tree, or some other object. You will see an upside down image of it on the paper screen!

6 Ask a friend to help put the coat over your head and around the sides and bottom of the box. No light should get in!

5 Hold the box up to your eyes with the tracing paper facing you. Don't press it up to your face, though.

It's a Fact!

Rays of light bounce off the object at which you are pointing the pinhole. These rays carry a picture of it through the pinhole. As these light rays come through the hole they cross over, and so your picture appears upside down. This is how real cameras see pictures, too. However, they have film inside them instead of tracing paper!

Your eye is just like a pinhole camera. Luckily your brain unscrambles the pictures you see so that they are the right way up.

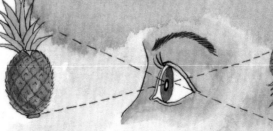

Paddle Power

This pefect paddleboat will make bathtime much more fun! You will need to find two old pens which are of similar length and weight. Your boat will offer another way of seeing Newton's Third Law of Motion in action (see page 4).

What you will need:
- 1 small, empty plastic bottle with a lid
- Scissors
- 2 old ballpoint or felt-tip pens
- Tape
- Rubber band

1

Cut a section out of the bottle as shown. Do not throw away the bit you have cut out.

2

Tape the pens to the sides of the bottle. Half of each one should stick out beyond the end of the bottle.

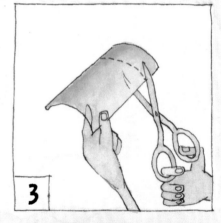

3

Cut a piece of plastic from the strip you have kept. It should be as long as the pen ends and just a bit narrower than the gap between them.

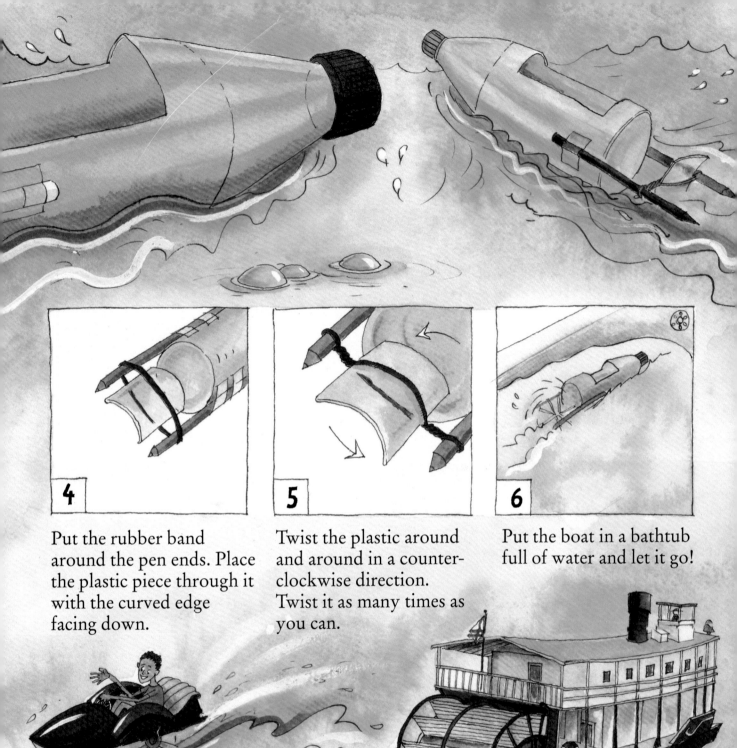

4 Put the rubber band around the pen ends. Place the plastic piece through it with the curved edge facing down.

5 Twist the plastic around and around in a counter-clockwise direction. Twist it as many times as you can.

6 Put the boat in a bathtub full of water and let it go!

Wheels in the Water

Steam engines for ships were first used in paddleboats. The engine turned two massive paddle wheels. The trouble was that these paddle steamers were not much good on the open ocean. When there was rough weather, the waves lifted one wheel out of the water while the other one was completely submerged. This strained the engine badly. When **propellers** were invented, they were used instead of paddle wheels because they didn't waste as much of the engine's energy.

Great Gliders!

You could make a few of these cool catapult contraptions and race them with your friends. After you've made one plane, feel free to experiment with different shapes for wings!

What you will need:
- 1 large piece of thin styrofoam from a food package
- A marker
- Tape
- Scissors
- Glue or double-sided tape
- 1 paper fastener
- Reusable poster putty
- Rubber band

1

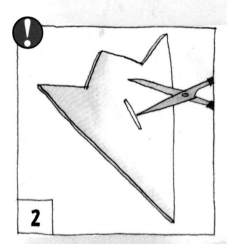

2

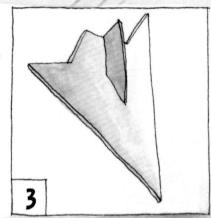

3

Look carefully at these shapes. Then draw them on the styrofoam.

Cut out the shapes from the first step. Cut a slit in the main body as seen above.

Push the tail piece through the slit so that it stands upright.

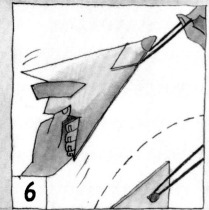

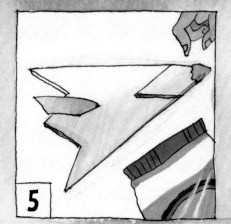

Push the paper fastener through the main body near the nose. Fold the legs of the fastener back. Make sure the pin head is not too tight against the styrofoam.

Using glue or double-sided tape, add the small body piece on top of the fastener's legs. Mold a piece of poster putty around the glider's nose to weigh it down.

Place the rubber band around the head of the fastener. Pull it tight and launch your glider!

The Wonderful Wright Brothers

The first people to create a flying machine with an engine,
Wilbur and Orville Wright, started with gliders!
They created some amazing contraptions.
Some of them travelled as far as 650 feet (200 m).
They all relied on the wind for power.

The ingenious Wright brothers eventually came up
with a flying machine with an engine and two propellers.
On December 17, 1903, it took off and flew about 130 feet
(40 m). It was the world's first powered flight.

Manic Messages

Build a nifty electrical circuit with two switches to control the flashing bulbs and send messages by Morse code. The complete code is on the opposite page. Send a friend into the next room with his half of the circuit. To receive a message, you need to hold down your switch while your friend taps his switch off and on to make the bulbs flash. Then you can send your answer while your friend holds his switch down.

1 Tape the batteries into two pairs. Tape them to the box lids. (Put the + and - together as shown.)

+ = positive
- = negative

2 Using the scissors, strip a little bit of plastic from each end of each piece of wire.

3 Push the screws through the tops of the lids. Tape the bulb holders to the lids.

WARNING!
You must NEVER experiment or play with the electricity that comes from an electrical socket.

5 Fix each end of one 6-foot (2 m) wire to the batteries with poster putty or plasticine.

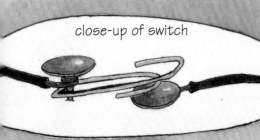

close-up of switch

switch

6 Use poster putty or plasticine to fix one 5-inch (12 cm) wire to each free end of the batteries. Curl the other end around a thumbtack. Push the thumbtack through a paper clip and into the cardboard.

7 Curl each end of the other 6-foot (2 m) wire under one screw of each bulb holder. Tighten the screws.

What you will need:

- 2 shoebox lids
- 4 1.5-volt batteries
- 2 2-volt or 2.5-volt lightbulbs in holders with screws
- 4 5-inch (12 cm) lengths of plastic-covered electrical wire
- 2 6-foot (2 m) lengths of plastic-covered electrical wire
- Scissors
- Reusable poster putty or plasticine
- Tape
- Screwdriver
- 4 thumbtacks
- 2 paper clips

4

Use the screwdriver to loosen the screws on each side of the bulb holders.

Dots and Dashes

Morse code was invented in 1838 by Samuel Morse. He sent a message in the form of electrical signals along a wire. He tapped out long and short sounds to represent different letters of the alphabet. You can do the same by making the lightbulbs flash quickly for a dot and longer for a dash.

A	·—
B	—···
C	—·—·
D	—··
E	·
F	··—·
G	——·
H	····
I	··
J	·———
K	—·—
L	·—··
M	——
N	—·
O	———
P	·——·
Q	——·—
R	·—·
S	···
T	—
U	··—
V	···—
W	·——
X	—··—
Y	—·——
Z	——··

8 Curl the end of a 5-inch (12 cm) wire around a thumbtack and then push it into the cardboard near the other thumbtack.

9 Curl the other end of the 5-inch (12 cm) wire under the screws on the other sides of the bulb holders.

Whizzy Whirler

This is a simple version of a helicopter. It can still fly high and fast, though!

What you will need:
- Thin cardboard (from a cereal box, for example)
- Pen or pencil
- Scissors
- Drinking straw
- Paper clip
- Tape

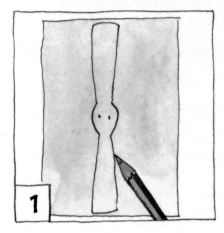

1. Draw this shape on the cardboard. Cut it out.

2. Uncurl the paper clip so that it just has one bend left. Push the ends through the dots in the middle of the propeller.

3. Push the ends down into the straw. Use tape to make the propeller extra secure.

4. Hold the straw between the palms of your hands. Rub your hands back and forth quickly. Then let the straw go with a throwing motion.

It's a Fact!

Compressed air helps a helicopter take off. As the blades, or rotors, whiz around, they push air down. This compresses the air underneath them. This compressed air pushes the helicopter upwards.

The Ingenious Leonardo

An amazing, early version of a helicopter was designed by Leonardo da Vinci during the fifteenth century. He was a painter, architect, musician, and inventor who drew all sorts of designs for many weird and wonderful devices. His airscrew was a corkscrew-shaped contraption. The screw turning would have made it climb upwards like a modern-day helicopter.

Sikorsky's Solution

The first helicopter was invented in 1907 by a Frenchman named Paul Cornu. It had two rotors and could rise about 5 feet (2 m) into the air. The trouble was that the body of the helicopter spun around, too, in the opposite direction than the wings! This problem is known as torque.

In 1939, a Russian called Igor Sikorsky designed a helicopter with a main rotor and one at the tail of the machine, too. This small rotor solved the problem of torque and kept the body of the helicopter from whirling around at the same time as the wings!

Read More

Hauser, Jill Frankel. *Gizmos & Gadgets: Creating Science Contraptions That Work (& Knowing Why)*. Charlotte, Vermont: Williamson Publishing Company, 1999.

Murphy, Glenn. *Inventions*. Insiders. New York: Simon & Schuster, 2009.

Sirrine, Carol. *Cool Crafts with Old Wrappers, Cans, and Bottles*. Green Projects for Resourceful Kids. Mankato, Minnesota: Capstone Press, 2010.

Glossary

atmosphere (AT-muh-sfeer) The layer of gases around an object in space. On Earth this layer is air.

barometer (buh-RAH-meh-tur) A tool used to measure air pressure, or the weight of air.

periscope (PER-uh-skohp) A tool that is used to see around corners, over barriers, or above the surface of the water.

propellers (pruh-PEL-erz) Paddlelike parts on an object that spin to move the object forward.

rain gauge (RAYN GAYJ) A tool for measuring how much rain has fallen.

reflects (rih-FLEKTS) Throws back light, heat, or sound.

Index

Web Sites

For Web resources related to the subject of this book, go to: www.windmillbooks.com/weblinks and select this book's title.